Edge of Wild

Encouragement for Foster Parents

Krystle Bowen

"These pages are filled with the hope and contagious passion that I have come to expect and appreciate in Krystle. She brings light to a hard and often ignored subject, challenging and encouraging those who are serious about their role in foster care."
- Adriel Booker
Author of Grace Like Scarlett

To Little Man and Sunshine
Thank you for teaching me how to love deeper

Learn to do good.
Seek justice.
Help the oppressed.
Defend the cause of orphans.

Isaiah 1:17

Introduction

Before you dive into this book I want you to know that I have prayed for you. I prayed for the hands that would thumb through this book and the lives they would touch. I prayed that no matter where you are in your foster care journey, you would find hope, encouragement and strength to press into the hard yet good things to come.

This book is a series of writings to take with you along your journey of foster care. There are invitations at the end of each section to dig a little deeper, and at the end of the book are some specific prayers you can utilize and a tangible way to remember the sweet kiddos who come into your care. These little resources are extra tools that I wish I would have had, but at the end of the day I just want you to feel encouraged as you read. This isn't homework. These words are my gift to you. They are my heart.

When we said yes to foster care it felt a little audacious and a little crazy. The anticipation of walking into the unknown always feels a little reckless. There are hard, painful moments in foster care and there are incredibly joy filled redemptive moments that always leave you feeling like you're on the edge of something…wild. Just know, you aren't alone.

"There are no safe paths in this part of the world. Remember you are over the Edge of the Wild now, and in for all sorts of fun wherever you go." J.R.R. Tolkien, <u>The Hobbit</u>

1

A Foster Parent Manifesto

I will be faithful with what is in front of me, even when I cannot see the finish line.

I will give up my need for control, even when nothing ever feels sure again.

I will surrender the need to know every detail before I show up.

I will move intentionally through my day as to not miss a moment where His grace might leak through.

I will move closer when I want to push away.

I will lay things down at the feet of the Father instead of carrying them around like a badge of burden.

Even if I never see good come from this, if I never glimpse redemption this side of heaven - I will remain.

I will embrace the chaos because that is where I am needed.

I will be a bridge and not an island.

Even when the storm is relentless and wreaks destruction all around me, I will hide myself in the only place I know that brings peace.

Even when things don't go as planned and my heart aches for justice - I will remain.

I will count all as a gift because there is treasure hidden to find if I am willing to dig.

I will submit to a continual death of myself in order to gain life in full.

Even when I cannot see any hope - I will remain.

I will trust, even when.

A Calling Into Something More

Definition of CALLING: a strong inner impulse toward a particular course of action especially when accompanied by conviction of divine influence

Several years ago our family knew there were things on the horizon, big life-changing things that we could only begin to guess at. Jesus was stirring our hearts, calling us to a life of more. Not more things, but more sacrifice. A life completely abandoned to Him and a willingness to go and do whatever was asked of us. I was ready to go. Let's move to Sudan, sell all of our things, and live in a grass hut! Let's adopt from another country. Let's do something crazy.

Something crazy was coming, but it was far closer to home. As we continued to pray through the stirrings of our heart, we began to realize that the topic of adoption kept rising to the surface. I've been open to adoption my whole life, within specific parameters (international, closed adoption, a girl under age one, and so on). I was willing to go the adoption route, but only if it looked exactly how I envisioned it, a scenario where I was least likely to get hurt. I was also very adamant I could never foster but along our journey into the world of adoption, that is exactly where we found ourselves.

I was scared out of my ever-loving mind. This wasn't what I envisioned when I knew our family was heading into deeper waters. This felt more reckless than moving across country - it was too close, too personal, too proximate. It was not neat and tidy and comfortable like I planned.

I could never love a child and give that child back.

I remember sitting in my living room venting to God about this tug and this fear of loving and losing and I heard His voice gently remind me, "This is not about you. These children need to be loved and let go, more than you need to protect your heart from loss." When we said we would be willing to move forward one step at a time and say yes to God no matter what, we meant it. Was it worth the obedience, to trust in the unknown and move into what God was calling us to?

Jesus says in John 12:24, *"Anyone who holds on to life just as it is destroys that life. But if you let it go, reckless in love, you'll have it forever, real and eternal."* MSG

I don't know what your call looks like, or what made you say yes to foster care, but I believe this calling is one of eternal ramifications - there is deeper work here than what we see and I am willing to give up the life of comfort for it - being a little reckless with my love.

This life of foster care feels scary at times because, at our most vulnerable, we are afraid to love and lose again and the grief that comes with each goodbye is almost too much to bear. When I feel afraid to step out, I have to remind myself that Jesus has gone before and is with me in the unknown parts that lie ahead. Trusting Jesus is what brings life and allows me to fall deeper in love with Him.

I want you to pick the scariest part of your current situation...an impending court date, a big meeting or maybe a reunification on the horizon. Maybe everything feels scary right now, whatever it is I want you to write it out on the journal page. I want you to write it all down and then I want you to read it aloud and then I want you to commit to trusting Jesus with it, even when it doesn't feel like you can.

Why

"My favorite part about being a foster brother is caring for kids. The hardest part is getting them to be good listeners."- Jack, age 9

I don't know about you, but I often get asked why we said yes to foster care. The truth is, there are any number of reasons we chose foster care. We have a safe home and kids need a safe place to land. The shortage of foster parents is a national crisis and we couldn't pretend we didn't know about it.

The reasons not to do foster care were mostly selfish. The bottom line is we as Christians must be Kingdom minded. We must remember there is more at stake here than what we see and if we are willing to step into this mess and meet people where they are broken and in desperate need, the impact we have will be eternal. We know there are precious lives at stake. We know there are lives that are hurting and need the love of Jesus, just like we do - and, at the end of the day, that is what we want: to see God move in a powerful way, to break bondages, and to restore families and bring about a healing that has eternal ramifications.

Simply put, we want our lives to point to Jesus in all that we do and foster care is just one way to do that. The posture we take and our willingness to say yes to it opens doors and creates space for God to move. I am just as damaged as the next person and am no better than the parents of these children who have lost the right to parent for a season - I have just met grace in Jesus and I am compelled to live out of that grace - pouring it on in the places most are afraid to go.

My why may look a little different than yours, but I know at the heart of it lies your desire to be Jesus to a world in desperate need. We can only say so much with our words; it's our actions that change the course of time and the lives we encounter along the way. When I get lost in the madness of the system or I am overwhelmed at the challenges I face parenting a child in care, I have to remember my why. I have to go back to the deeper reason I do what I do. If I don't, I lose sight of it. I try to manufacture strength on my own and I end up worn and tired.

Ephesians 3:7 *"By God's grace and mighty power, I have been given the privilege of serving him by spreading this Good News."* NLT

Being a foster parent is hard. This is maybe one of the hardest things we have ever done, and in our weakest moments we need to remember why we are doing this. When I remember the why, I remember I am not alone and I remember to draw upon God's strength and not my own. I want to be called deeper into Grace and God's plan for my life. I want my life to be a manifestation of God's grace and mercy in all that I do.

On this journal page, write down your why. It could be because you are a relative and there was no one else to provide care. It could be because you saw the need and had an extra bed, maybe you are hopeful to adopt someday or maybe you just felt like there was no reason to keep saying no. Whatever your why, write it down. This page and the previous should become reference points for you when you need to remember your WHO - Jesus, and your WHY.

Shock and Awe

"On those hard days when I want to quit I look at these children and remember how great the father's love has been lavished upon me. So I lean into Jesus trusting he'll give me the strength for each day."
- Crystal, Oregon Foster and Adoptive Parent

One month in and I find myself in a time warp. What day is it? How many appointments do we have this week? You can go to as many trainings and classes as they require of you and still be completely clueless when reality sets in. Our first placement was an infant boy with huge blue saucers for eyes and a mop of brown hair. He was delightful as much as he was exhausting. I'd forgotten about the whole "night waking" thing and all the darn bottles. We'd been provisionally certified on a Tuesday at 4pm and got the call to take him 24 hours later. Our friends and family swooped in to gather the supplies needed and we were up and running, but neither fully up nor running. I went to church that night because I always went to church on Wednesday. I think I was afraid to be home with this stranger baby and my three boys so I just drove there. I was also in a bit of shock to be honest. I marched upstairs with a baby in a car seat and a half-empty bottle in hand, greeted by handfuls of teenagers giddy to see this adorable bundle. I made a new bottle and settled in on the couch while the student worship band played.

The words came as I rocked him to sleep, "You're a Good Good Father, that's who you are and I'm loved by you." I couldn't stop the tears that fell down my face. It was all so much in that moment.

The Good Father who cares for me and cares for this precious boy that I was parenting at the moment.

His situation, his future - all of it unknown to everyone but God. He loved this little boy more than any person on earth and He knew what lay in store for Him. There was a peace that overcame me as I sat there - recognizing I was living out my statement to say "yes" to whatever was ahead and my yes, in that moment, was this baby, and this baby was loved and cared for. Everything he lacked on this earth was being provided for him in heaven, and I trusted God to be faithful.

I choose to believe in a Good Father who knows what lies ahead for these children, however scary it may be. I believe He is trustworthy and I am confident that no one cares more for them than He does. If you are struggling with the unknown future of the children you have or are caring for - you need to know there is a Father in heaven who cares deeply for these children, they are not forgotten and their future, while unknown to you, is not a mystery to Jesus.

Romans 8:31-39 says *"So, what do you think? With God on our side like this, how can we lose? If God didn't hesitate to put everything on the line for us, embracing our condition and exposing himself to the worst by sending his own Son, is there anything else he wouldn't gladly and freely do for us? And who would dare tangle with God by messing with one of God's chosen? Who would dare even to point a finger? The one who died for us – who was raised to life for us! – is in the presence of God at this very moment sticking up for us."* MSG

How grateful I am to know that not only does our Father intercede, stand up for and love us, but that He would do anything for us. Spend some time today in quiet prayer, reflecting on Romans 8 and who God is to you and to the child(ren) you care for. Use the journaling page to make this passage personal to you and to the kids in your care.

Brokenness

I have been broken in a thousand ways and yet I keep returning to the thing that breaks me. There is something in this space that is holy and sacred and I am undone.

I was a resister for so long - why hurt? Why sacrifice? Why be burdened? Why add more to our full plates, change our family dynamic and enter a system of utter chaos?

I'm good here, where I am, thanks.

I am being challenged no doubt. I give monthly to multiple causes. I have been on trips to third world countries for goodness sake. I am not ignorant to the needs around me.

The whisper of "I am willing to say yes to anything" can be an empty and meaningless phrase if it comes with an addendum, a hidden clause that says, "Anything but ____."

Maybe it's the unknown "but"- though it's there somewhere: but the timing, lack of space, but our finances, our security, whatever the "but" is...

People are doing awful things and are caught in vicious cycles of addiction, abuse, poverty and illness, and they do awful things when they are stuck and hurting. And then there are the children.

These children are born into the arms of addiction, abuse, poverty and illness. They need a voice to speak up for them. The church needs to link arms with the parents who cannot care for the lives they deeply love, yet cannot in this moment care for.

We must learn to see people the way Jesus sees them and be willing to say, "However long it takes we believe in you. Whatever you may need to make this work, I'm with you."

If we are not willing to walk with people in their mess, see them how Jesus sees them and link arms with those that are hurting, Christianity becomes a banner we wave instead of a lifestyle we live. This is messy and there are no black and white answers that we sometimes desperately want. We need to continue stepping into the hard places, speaking up for the ones who need a voice, and being an advocate for the children lost in the static.

Sometimes people don't even know there is a need. I didn't realize how bad the foster care situation was until I was exposed to it. Today I want you to speak up. Be an advocate for the system in some way. Host a Facebook Live to answer questions, open your home up and do an informal recruitment meeting, find a local non-profit to lend your voice to. Spur others on to do a good work, whether that is fostering or supporting those that do. Pick one thing and speak out. Sometimes people just need a nudge, they need to be exposed to what is happening in their own neighborhoods. Jot down as many ideas as you can think of, small or big.

As Jesus Does

I have never felt closer to Jesus than when I've been rocking a baby whose mother is doing her fighting best to get him back. I've never felt nearer to the clear Biblical call to lay down my life for the sake of others than when I'm comforting a little girl who cries out for her mommy at night, unable to fall asleep unless my hand is touching hers.

I become broken and undone and isn't that who Jesus was for me?
Wasn't he wounded and crushed for me?

Wasn't it the broken that He became broken for?

Isaiah 53:5 *"But he was pierced for our rebellions, crushed for our sins. He was beaten so we could be whole. He was whipped so we could be healed."* NLT

If I am to live like Jesus then wouldn't my life speak of brokenness as well?

Matthew 25:35-40 *"For I was hungry, and you fed me. I was thirsty and you gave me a drink. I was a stranger, and you invited me into your home. I was naked, and you gave me clothing. I was sick, and you cared for me. I was in prison, and you visited me."* NLT

In her book "The Broken Way", Ann Voskamp says, "Never be afraid of broken things - because Christ can redeem anything."

The practice of communion is a reminder of Christ's redeeming love in that He was broken for us. It is also a sacred moment we share in community in which we are called to follow Christ into the brokenness of one another.

We walk through a hurting world, allowing ourselves to break again and again. We allow our pride, entitlement, security, routine...all of it to be broken again because the people in this messy world are worth it. We pray for others to become aware, to be deeply affected and profoundly impacted so that collectively we can change the world.

Take the following journal pages to reflect on your own brokenness. How do you feel about the brokenness you are witnessing as a foster parent? Can you remember a time when someone moved toward your brokenness, and what that did for you?

Scripture

Each of my children have a Bible verse. My husband and I picked out a verse for each of them after they were a few years old and we saw their personalities shine. We read over several scriptures for each until we felt we'd found the right ones. Once we'd chosen, we had a graphic designer create a beautiful print that we hung in their rooms and we began to pray their verses over them each night.

We chose verses that we felt were not only fitting to them currently, but would also be true about them in the future, their verses becoming a part of their identity.

A few days after our first placement, I asked my kids if we should pick a verse for this little boy and they were so excited to do so. My oldest immediately said, "Jeremiah 33:3."

"Call to me and I will answer you, I will tell you great and unsearchable things you do not know." NIV

We began praying this over him every night, that wherever he went from our home, wherever his life took him, he would have something inside him that begs to search for more. He would not be able to settle until he has sought out Jesus for his answers, because we have a faithful Father who will meet every need. He may never know how he was loved by us, we may never see where life takes him, but whether or not we are a part of his life in the future we know that God has his hands on him and will be faithful to meet him where he is.

Picking verses for your foster children is a powerful way to speak over their lives and, depending on their age, they may remember those words for the rest of their lives. Today I want you to begin praying about a verse to pray over your children, whether they are your forever children or foster children. Over the course of the next few days continue praying and sharing with your spouse about possible verses you can claim as theirs and share with your children the why behind it. It has become a powerful time in our bedtime routine. Once you have picked your verses, write them here alongside their names. This will be a precious reference point for years to come.

Isolation

It's kind of amazing, isn't it, how alone you can feel when you're busier than you've ever been? You meet with more people for appointments than you would in an entire year otherwise and, whether you're introverted or extroverted, you are feeling the "too much" of it all.

This is often the space foster care lands you in. You are not alone and yet you feel alone, because it seems nobody on earth can relate to what you're going through. Other foster parents are the only thing that comes close and, unless you find a few healthy foster parents to encourage you and vent alongside, or you find yourself in an unhealthy space of internalizing or just complaining to anyone who lends an ear.

Our first placement got sick shortly after he came to us. He was 7 months old, and he would cycle through sicknesses for the remainder of his stay.

Of course, he was so kind and shared with our other children which made for a season that we still refer to as "the plague." One sickness in particular stands out. It was towards the end of my oldest son's basketball season and during a weeklong event at our church with one of my favorite speakers. I'd been looking forward to both the final game and a week of challenging and inspiring messages. Instead, I was stuck at home with a baby and the lovely disease that is "Hand, Foot and Mouth." Starting with the baby, every three days like clockwork, one of our kids got it. This meant that by the time the baby was ready to go back out into society, I was still at home with the next sick kid. Two weeks. Two weeks of being stuck at home with sick kids, one after the next. Missing basketball, my son getting an award, the entire week at church, and so on and so on. I wish I could say I handled that with grace and dignity, but I am not sure I showered much during that time, and I was pretty angry.

I hadn't sought out isolation; it had come knocking at my door. Social media was a window into the outside world, but nothing ever replaces human contact and conversation, and even introverted souls need that as well.

This is an extreme example. But the truth is, foster care on its own is isolating. The first rule about a foster care case is... you do not talk about a foster care case. The second rule of a foster care case is...well you get the picture. You can't really talk about what's going on, you often don't have a clue what's going on, and it's an incredibly layered world that rarely makes sense. It causes you to rearrange your life, and that alone can be isolating. There will be times of forced isolation that you will have to push through, believing there is an end in sight, and there will be seasons of emotional isolation you must learn to navigate.

I have learned two things I need in order to keep sane: avoid isolation and take care of myself.

I need a regular night out with a few friends. Maybe it's a movie, dinner, or coffee, but whatever it is, I have to schedule it, and make it a priority. I need to do this every other week at least.

I need fresh air. Yes, I am often alone when I do this, but being outside for a walk or run or hike somehow makes me feel more connected to the world outside of my home. For some this is easy, but I am a "hunker down and hibernate" type of a person when life gets heavy and if I am not careful I will lose myself and my motivation. But, if I am consistent in these things, no matter the juggling I have to do in order to make it happen, my mental state is in a far better place.

What about you? What things do you need to make sure are in place to fight against isolation, both emotionally and physically? Identify what those things are for you, write them down and make it a priority to be consistent with them. And if you're really brave, identify someone you can ask to hold you accountable.

Tribe

You probably know that old saying, "It takes a village to raise a child." I think a more accurate statement would be, "It takes a village to make sure parents don't go crazy trying to parent their children." The village, in my opinion, is far more about the support system you have, than making sure your kid has an extra set of eyes on them.

Village. Tribe. Council. Kibbutz. Whatever you call it, you need it.

Shoot, even Jesus had his small group of friends who were privy to the inner layers of his heart and life. He kept it fairly small and casual, nothing fancy.
If you are fostering, a village is a must. You just can't thrive without one. You can survive, sure, but there won't be much left of you, and that's really not the point of it all. If you are wearing yourself out and calling it "living for Jesus," you're lying to yourself with false humility. Ouch.

We simply cannot do Kingdom work without the support and care of people who understand what we are doing, why we are doing it, and show up anyway. Like I mentioned yesterday, isolation happens sometimes without us even trying, and we have to fight back any way we can.

If you don't already have a village of people you can call on at a moment's notice for prayer, a grocery run when the kids have the pukes, or a coffee run when you are stuck inside for 12 days because Hand, Foot and Mouth has taken up residence and will not leave, you need to find one. No, it's not easy, but you get to decide. You can keep treading water, or jump out and grab a lifeline.

Do you already have a village of people who support your family as you foster? If so, are you living in community with them to maintain a healthy support system? If not, start today. If you don't feel like you have a village, ask yourself why. If you've been waiting for people to come to you, maybe it's time to reach out and create something for yourself. Jot down some names, or remind yourself who is already in your tribe and spend some time writing down your thankfulness for them!

Respite

According to Merriam-Webster, the definition of respite is "a period of temporary delay, an interval of rest or relief."

I have noticed a common theme among foster parents. They do not schedule respite care; or they wait until they feel like they are going to quit fostering and then get respite.

Is it pride or guilt or something else that keeps one from asking for help?

This was how I approached respite with our first placement - weary from sleepless nights and shock of how the system worked took its toll, but I waited until I was flat out on the verge of a breakdown before I asked for help.

Initially I thought, "Well, I signed up for this, so I need to handle it," but as time has passed and I've gained more wisdom, I see it as a necessary part of our rhythm.

We've become proactive in scheduling rest for our family, and we remain healthy instead of burning out and then begging for help.

For us it looks like scheduling once-a-month respite weekends for our family. A trusted friend or family member takes our little one for 1-2 nights and allows our family a time of rest together. This has made all the difference. Our little one is fine, has some extra fun, and we are able to return to fostering with renewed energy. We always love picking our kids up after a time away, happy to see them and enter into routine again. We love the moments we spend with our forever children, checking in with them to see how they are doing and getting a pulse on where they are at. This regular routine has been a game changer.

Sometimes it's not that we need a break from this child or children; it's more that we need a break from the emotion it takes to parent them. Parenting a child in care requires more of you than parenting your own children. The emotion involved in fostering children takes its toll and manifests itself in physical forms as well as spiritual and you need breaks from it.

Jesus often withdrew for respite. It was on a regular basis, not just when he was feeling tapped. The regular removal of himself allowed for him to continue his good hard work:

Luke 5:15 *"But Jesus often withdrew to the wilderness for prayer."* NLT

This is **Jesus** and he needed rest often, not sometimes, not when forced or when at his wits end. If we are to model ourselves after Jesus and he needed a break from it all, we might want to pay attention here.

Model yourselves after Jesus.

If you have people who have offered to help, have you utilized them? If not, schedule a time of respite today.

If you don't already have someone you can call, pray about some options. Call up a few people and be willing to ask for help. There may be those willing, who are waiting for you! Do you utilize respite while fostering? If not, spend some time journaling about why you don't. If you do, reflect on your feelings during and after those times of rest.

Bio Kids

As parents our biggest concern is how often our family choices impact our children. We make choices we believe are best for our family, and our children learn to ride the waves along with us. Sometimes we do this with eyes shut tightly and hope we don't screw them up completely in the process.

When we said yes to foster care, we knew it would impact our bio kids We just didn't know how.

We expected most of the results to be negative and prepared ourselves for the worst. At times it's been rough. Foster care can be hard, it's a messy broken system, and it often doesn't feel like things will get fixed this side of heaven. The selfish nature is also alive and well in all ages and that can be magnified in stressful situations.

What we hadn't expected are all the positive ways we've seen it impact our kids.

Their little worlds have been expanded, they see firsthand the need right in their home, and they become part of the answer to it. We've been able to teach our kids what it looks like to live selflessly and to be aware of others' needs in such a tangible way. The other night our oldest had a meltdown. He wanted to be the only one to push our new placement on a swing. He wanted Supreme Big Brother rights and wasn't willing to share. I mean, our kids were fighting over who got to help the most! They don't skip a beat welcoming a new sibling into the fold, even on days when it's hard. They seem to adjust far quicker to the extra person in our home than we do.

I think perhaps people use the question of how fostering will affect their bio kids as an excuse not to do it. There are a million reasons to say no to hard things, even scary things, but we are modeling for our own children what it is like to live a different kind of life. We are just going to do things a little differently than the world is. We may give up a typical schedule and lifestyle but this is what our family is called to and that includes our children.

When I talk to other people about this part of fostering I say, "It is absolutely scary but we don't ever want fear to control our decision making."

1 John 4:17b *"There is no room in love for fear. Well-formed love banishes fear. Since fear is crippling, a fearful life, fear of death, fear of judgment, is not one fully formed in love."* MSG

Are you holding back because of fear? Ask God to search your heart for anything that might be holding you back and call out the fear in your life. Ask God to remove that fear and give you boldness and trust and then step out of the boat and into a deeper calling of trust. Write it out, all the things you are holding back from in fear, and then ask a friend to hold you accountable in pushing past the fear into faith.

Tension

There is a heart wrenching tension you must live within to be a foster parent.

We must parent like we will have these children forever. We teach them boundaries in order to create safety, we establish routines to foster trust and security, and we model a healthy functioning family system. At the same time, we must hold loosely to them, recognizing our role is most likely temporary. We do not have the final say, and we must come to grips with the reality that all we have established may unravel the moment they leave our care.

You cannot go half-heartedly into this though; you must be willing to walk that tension because the goal is to discover what is best for these children. And what is best, is almost never clean or simple - it's tension-filled. They need you to attach, parent, guide, correct, comfort, soothe, and restore in this season. It is ultimately what sets them up for future success. We can see evidence of this in the lives of the children who have been reunited or adopted and we can read all the hard evidence in textbooks. This is what the children need, but it will not be easy.

Your investment in the temporary, you see, will have profound impact on their future.

Walking this tight rope looks like a lot of learning on the fly, making mistakes and trying again. You will not get it right every time. You will push away when you need to pull in, you will doubt your parenting when you need to trust your instincts. You will step on toes of family members and possibly even cause drama you don't intend. You will seek to do your very best and then know that, once they leave your care, things will never again be the same. That tight-rope walking requires a steady focus on your why and a daily commitment to the task at hand. This is the hard truth of foster care, the risk we take when we say yes and the reality we face daily. Instead of running from it, Jesus asks us to move towards it. Move towards the tension, the hard parts and the suffering.

Matt 16:25 *"Anyone who intends to come with me has to let me lead. You're not in the driver's seat, I am. Don't run from suffering; embrace it. Follow me and I'll show you how..."* MSG

Start a prayer journal - for you and the child(ren) in your care. Think the tension that exists in your current situation, write it down. This is not just a place to pray about it, but also to help you track your commitment and restate your motive to love through prayer.

Roller Coaster

I am afraid of heights. I will avoid sitting up high on bleachers and, if necessary, I will sit on my butt and slide down, one by one, until I safely reach the bottom. We were talking with our close friends about a possible Yosemite Half Dome hike a few years back, and, after I watched every video out there and completely freaked myself out, I said a solid and firm "No."

I do enjoy roller coasters. They go so fast, I can't really tell what's happening and it's over before you know it. Lately though, they make me nauseous. Maybe I'm getting old, but the last time I was at a theme park full of coasters I was just sure I was going to pass out or throw up. I eventually decided to participate with our group and sure enough was on the verge of passing out, but I was convinced if I let myself keel over, my "friends" would post a picture of me before offering assistance.

Foster parenting is like the biggest, bumpiest, sometimes nauseating roller coaster I've ever been on. It has some really exciting moments and the feeling you're on top of the world. The moment you think you know what's next, it does some sort of 360 upside down corkscrew move you didn't see coming and you feel like you're going to lose your cookies.

Being able to adapt on the fly isn't a skill everyone has, but it's one I know I've needed to work on since fostering. Knowing there are twists and turns ahead is helpful and expecting them is part of the ride.
Basically, everything you think you know is coming will change. There are no guarantees and stuff changes so fast it's pointless trying to keep up. You just have to close your eyes, lean back, and take the ride as it comes. The highs are worth the ride, even if you sometimes puke in the end.

There are so many moving parts in a case and we aren't always privy to the inner workings. Being flexible and gracious in change is important, but so is being able to laugh when things get too crazy. Laughing might turn to crying, and in hard cases it's hard to find happy moments; but if you can learn to laugh and enjoy the ride it will take a lot more weight off your shoulders.

I want you to do something fun. You might not be able to hop on a theme park ride but I want you to seek out something fun today. Don't give me excuses, just do it. It doesn't have to be a big deal, maybe you ride the cart like a kid after you've finished grocery shopping or you eat ice cream for dinner - whatever seems fun or silly to you - do it. We have to find some light-hearted moments in the midst of the heaviness if we want to keep our hearts soft and stress levels low. Write down what you did and some more ideas for the future. And if you can go ride a roller coaster today, by all means do it.

The System

I remember learning from our foster parent training how many people are involved in a child's life. Outside of the family and foster family there are any number of caseworkers, therapists, attorneys, counselors, CASA's, doctors, and teachers. It's a massive web of programs, procedures and paperwork, and at the center of it are real human lives with a lot at stake.

Navigating the systems can be frustrating and exhausting. Your foster child is your world and their life takes you a million directions any given day but, to caseworkers, it's another file in a stack of many. This isn't to say these hard-working people don't care, it is just the reality of what their job entails.

Finding your firm, but gracious voice is necessary to stay sane and keep your heart in the right spot.

It is okay to get mad. Not everybody you deal with is going to be awesome. You won't always see eye to eye and you will have harder personalities to work with. It is okay to speak up and speak out and there are times when you are the only sane voice in the room. Your job is to advocate for these children, and that might mean ruffling feathers to get what is needed for the kids. So don't ever be tempted to roll over and play dead, but I am also suggesting we temper our righteous anger with love.

There are days where I am flat out infuriated by the "system" and the seeming lack of understanding. I don't agree with the decisions being made and the course that is being taken. It is not easy to show up and be kind all of the time. I know I may not always agree with choices made on behalf of these kids, and

I am reminded I'm not in control of every outcome. But I am in control of how I handle the situation.

To keep myself sane, focused on my why, and adaptable, I ask myself over and over again "How can I show grace in this situation?" NT Wright asks the question, *"What would it mean to reflect God's generous love despite the pressure and provocation, despite your own anger and frustration?"*

Sometimes I think I need to carry that on a card with me wherever I go, put it on the fridge, stick it on the mirror and write it on my hand. So instead of giving in to my cynicism, I take deep breaths, show up, and show love.

It is easy to only see things from our perspective and forget there are real people doing a hard job on the other side of this. This is important. I want you to do something for your local child welfare office. Bring by some bagels and cream cheese or a few dozen flowers. Write a thoughtful card and drop it off, do something to brighten their day (yes even if you're ticked off at the moment). One of my foster mama friends raised money on Facebook to buy several Keurig machines for our local child welfare office because we all know coffee is life.

Choose love and show love today in a tangible way.

You are on the same team. Take some time to write out your current feelings and some ways you can move toward the funk. It will be worth it.

In the Face of Pain

You don't love me!
You're not my Mom!

Those are the words being hurled at me from the backseat as
we drive home from a family visit.

One of our caseworkers told me the grief children experience
after a parental visit is as though their family has died, and they
repeat this sometimes weekly. This kind of grief cripples the
strongest of adults. The fact that children are facing this over
and over again is heart wrenching.

Every time she said something hurtful to me, I would repeat "I
do love you, no matter what," even while tears stream down
my face. Those hurtful words directed at me are a direct result
of the pain she's going through and the lack of control and
coping mechanisms, and while I know it's not personal, it sure
feels that way.

Again and again I say, "no matter what."

When we get home, I get out of the car and sit next to her seat.
I take her face in my hands and I look her in the eyes.

"I love you. No matter what"

She sighs and says, "I love you too."

It is downright hard to keep loving when you are the recipient of the manifestation of pain. Jesus shows us in scripture how to respond with compassion again and again, and He's the one I must lean on in these moments. I don't know what kind of pain you've endured physically or emotionally because of the kids you have cared for, but I do know it hurts and it is unlike any other kind of pain because it is all encompassing. All at once you are hurt for yourself, for the family that lost this child, and for the child who has to endure the trauma they have endured without the coping skills they need.

These moments are the moments when pushing away is easier than pulling close. It is not easy to move towards a child when they are acting out, either in anger or defiance. I would just as soon avoid them altogether in those moments to be honest. We ourselves can be angry and selfish and in our hurt we act in ways that harm others. Jesus remains with us during these moments and models for us what it is like to be present in pain.

The next time you'd rather push away, pull in close and be part of the healing (both for them and you).
How does Jesus respond to you when you are whiny, angry, hurting or sad? Where do you see Jesus pulling you close during the more difficult parts of your day? Take some time to reflect on His nature. What other scriptures, moments or thoughts stand out to you?

Philippians 4:8-9 *"Summing it all up, friends, I'd say you'll do best by filling your minds and meditating on things true, noble, reputable, authentic, compelling, gracious—the best, not the worst; the beautiful, not the ugly; things to praise, not things to curse. Put into practice what you learned from me, what you heard and saw and realized. Do that, and God, who makes everything work together, will work you into his most excellent harmonies."* MSG

Wounded Birds

We came upon an injured robin at our doorstep. He'd been hopping along, but as Trevor grew closer and he did not fly away, we saw his wing was damaged. I quickly typed into my phone search bar "what to do with an injured bird" and we placed him on a towel in a box very gently and closed the lid. I called our local wildlife rescue and they asked us to bring him in. Our boys hopped in the car with my husband and they made the trek 45 minutes away.

That might seem like a lot for a bird, but we felt it was important to teach our boys that we care for animals too, and a suffering bird matters, and that there are really cool places that exist to rescue and rehabilitate animals from the wild. They handed the box over and Trevor took them for an ice cream treat for a job well done. I messaged the refuge the following day, hoping for an update on Mr. Robin. Unfortunately it wasn't what I'd hoped for. He had suffered a severe compound fracture in addition to a dislocated wing and couldn't be saved. While we were so sad, we were glad the little guy didn't suffer more, as I'm sure a cat would have gotten to him quickly.

It didn't really end the way I had hoped or wished for, but if we had known he wouldn't make it, we would have still picked him up and driven him to get care, we would have still taught our boys to be responsible and caring, and to seek help for wounded ones. Despite the ending we did not plan for, the two hour trip on a Sunday afternoon wasn't wasted. That day was the first day I'd really thought hard about when we have to say goodbye to kids. The reality is we will say goodbye. It could be rather soon or it could be awhile from now, but that day will come. We'd like to think that we would be hopeful about where they go from here, we'd wish for the best possible outcome for them and we'd like to see a future before them that is full of joy and possibility and healing. The truth is, we may not like where they go from here. We may have concerns and worries about where they go when they leave us and those outcomes are beyond our control. You want, ever so much, for this to be a bridge between brokenness and healing, but the reality is you may never get to see that healing. You may not be privy to that information or it may not bring the wholeness you prayed for in your time. We cannot say yes to foster care if we can only handle the "good" goodbyes, the ones that reunite a healthy family that has worked hard, or the new forever family that offers so much love and redemption you couldn't have asked for more. These happen, but the other kind happen to. The returns to family that make you question your role or the system over and over again. The returns that make you weep in fear for the future of the child who you loved while they were in your care. Some returns do not offer the hope of healing you so desperately want to see. Would we say no if we knew when they left us it was not for what we hoped? If we could have seen the future and saw the continued heartache and loss a child would endure, would we have still stepped in to offer comfort and peace in the midst of that storm? Absolutely. Because that is not the reason you foster. It is not just about the happy endings we can see. It's much bigger than that, there is a bigger story you are a part of, a bigger Hope to hold on to. That is what you cling to when the water seems muddy and you're broken for these children. You must cling to the hope that the story doesn't end there. So you love. You love hard and big, and you provide comfort and safety and you go all in because you do not know what may lie ahead, you battle for them while they are in your care. You trust as they leave your nest that there is Someone who watches over them and cares for them more than you ever possibly could and He knows all about redemption and restoration and He is still writing those stories...

Our family loves the Jesus Storybook Bible. We love how it weaves our stories into the story of Jesus and all humanity. If you don't own it I would recommend picking it up and making it a part of your daily routine. The kids in our care are a part of a beautiful story and if they only ever hear about it in our homes, I trust Jesus will hide it in their hearts for when they are grown.

Fostering the Whole Family

"There are so many problems in this world. There is homelessness, domestic violence, child abuse, addiction...Foster Care is a crossroads where you see all of those things, and you have an opportunity to make an impact. Not only in the life of a child, but in the lives of the entire family."
- Leah, Oregon Foster and Adoptive Mom

A lot of people get into foster care for the children. They feel like, "If I can advocate for this child I can make a difference!"

And that is true, but the primary goal of foster care is reunification if at all possible, so unless we take into consideration the entire family and not just the child, we are doing a disservice to these kids.

That may sound harsh, but let me confess I am talking mostly to myself. I knew this reality with our first placement. It was easy to wrap around his mom, to love her, to encourage her, to support her. I had no problem with that. It was second nature to me. I didn't even have to think about it...I was doing it before I even realized it. Seeing her succeed as a mom was incredibly gratifying.

Not every go around will be this easy. We had a situation that was a little different in that we were supposed to be just a temporary home in the truest sense of the word temporary (I hear you giggling). The plan was for the little one we would take in, to quickly move to extended family.

When we first got the call and were told it would be one or two months tops, it felt easy, like absolutely we can just be the placeholder until this goes through! The fact that I don't work during the summer made this seem like a no-brainer.

As it unfolded, it was far more involved than we anticipated.

I went into Mama Bear mode. I thought and said things aloud that revealed my heart was not in the right place, not in a place of hoping for reunification. Things were revealed or not revealed to me, plans made against what we had worked out and I got mad. Real mad. I told God all about it and during a time in prayer I was reminded of why we got into this, reminded once again that this is not about me, and yes I am learning so much through this process. But what is the bottom line? Do I truly care for this entire family? I need to. I may not agree with how things are happening right now, I may not understand it at all, and I may feel less support than I did last time, because this is so much harder to explain...But if I am for this sweet precious soul, then I must be for the family and what's best for this little one, even if I don't understand.

To be sure, if I saw things happening that I thought were truly damaging, I would speak up, and, in cases where the reunification would be the most damaging of all, I would fight like mad for that not to happen. The reality here is that what I see is just the norm for the foster care process, and there's not much I can do about it. In my come-to-Jesus moment, I am once again faced with my failings as a human and my innate selfish nature. So I take a step back, let Jesus fix it, and do my best to love. I have been loved at my worst. Who am I to withhold that from others?

I know not every situation is the same, but most often we all have contact with bio parents or family. I want you to take a step towards them. I want you to decide to move close to them even if it is hard. Print off a bunch of candid photos you've captured of their child(ren), write a note about the daily routine, ask for pictures of themselves to be hung up at your house, do something to show them that you care and that you are for them. This was a game changer for the mom of our first placement. The love and support we showed her gave her confidence and courage to keep going and her reunification with her son is a result of that. Jot down your ideas for reference later.

Me Too

Sometimes I fear we believe we must have it figured out before we share.
We must have crossed through that middle space, now having clarity and beautiful perspective, before we can share about the depths through which we waded to get to that other side.

I love to read. The books I read, maybe a memoir or an intended encouragement, all look the same.
They have a beginning with some sort of challenge/road block/unexpected bump.
They have a middle that includes an inciting incident/come to Jesus/reckoning moment,
and an ending where it's either all wrapped up in a tidy bow or it's not.
Either way there is a beginning, middle, and end.

The authors share their struggle and the victory they found, in hopes that we might push through whatever we are facing to find that "promised land" as if saying...
"Look, over here it's better so keep going."

Sometimes I want to call BS.

I want to say, your story isn't mine and there is no guarantee I will find what you found in this lifetime so don't give me the steps, the outline, or the script.

Where are the stories of those in the thick of it, the ones who haven't reached the other side of the valley yet? Where are the stories that say, "I'm here in the middle and if you are too, let's do this together, because I haven't figured it out, but maybe we can together." Why doesn't anyone share that part?

Some days I see things clearly. I see a God who has ordained my every step and still allows me to choose the path I take. Ever patient in my choices, drawing me back to Him no matter which path I choose. Not a puppet master, but an artist who creates along the way - pursuing me as I pursue the higher calling on my life.

Some days I feel weighted. I feel as if I'm under water with barely enough strength to come up now and again for a deep breath that ensures I can last a little longer.
I don't quite see the point of it all. I don't want to be tested, used, or drawn in any which way.
I question telling God I would do ANYTHING He asked of me.
Every step feels heavy and without purpose other than to just survive.
What the heck am I doing anyway?

Of course, then I feel guilty for questioning anything at all, my doubts rising to the surface, making me feel fraudulent.
Because authenticity is to me as important as breath is to life, I find myself crippled at the thought of being fake.

So, how do I reconcile my wrestling on the hard days?
How do I give myself space to doubt and process it without feeling like I must have all the answers right then?

I am learning to give myself grace on the days that I doubt.
Learning that it's okay to wrestle with the hard stuff, and not having an answer for it at that moment doesn't make me fake but makes me real.

It's okay to shout ~~this year~~ today sucks, and still love Jesus.
It's okay to grumble and complain while also reading your Bible and telling Him you're kinda ticked off the way the weeks have gone, and you don't even feel like doing this, but you're doing it because you do believe He is faithful, despite the muddy waters you travel in.
I don't have it all figured out.

60

I have days where even the hard stuff feels purposeful.
And there are days when the hard stuff, no matter how big or small, feels completely pointless and I want to throw in the towel on this "upstream living."

I guess what this is...is a me too.

Feeling weighted? Me too.
Feeling like this is really hard? Me too.
Feeling like some days are easier than others, to live out this life in Christ, to be used and poured out in all ways? Me too.

I haven't arrived, nor do I think I will in this lifetime.
But I do believe that each moment that is hard, and each moment that is good, and each moment that is painful is doing something in me.
It's refining me and making me more like Christ, and, on the hardest of days, I still choose this over a life of not pursuing Him at all. Hardship produces qualities in you that no other experience can.
The tough stuff brings about things that cannot, in any other way, draw you into nearness with Christ.

I guess I'm thankful for those "reached-the-other-side stories" after all, otherwise I wouldn't know that statement to be true, and I wouldn't know there were others who had once said,

"Me too."

Be vulnerable today - share your journey with someone who may need to hear it. Brené Brown, author of multiple books, and a research professor at the University of Houston has spent 16 years studying courage and empathy. She says "True belonging only happens when we present our authentic, imperfect selves to the world, our sense of belonging can never be greater than our level of self-acceptance." Who are you going to share with today?

When You Want To Quit

There are days I want to quit. When the colds and sickness won't relent, when I am not sleeping at all, when the weight of it feels too heavy to bear. When I don't have a timeline and there are so many unknowns, the future can feel dim. The day to day navigation of the foster care world can wring out even the strongest of people.

I had been signed up for a half marathon race when we got a placement. The age of the child and timing of it was such that my training suffered and I pulled out. I was really upset. I felt like I had no time for myself, no margin for any sort of self care. In fact I just sat and cried for a long time after emailing the race director. I have this personality trait where I'd rather not even try, than be less than I'd hoped. Prideful much?!

The reality is, some days we cope with our situations better than others. Some days I am totally okay with this life and some days I struggle to make it to bedtime without a breakdown. It can just be so very isolating and there is nothing I can do to change it, nothing anyone else can do. It's just a reality.

So I said I wanted to quit. When our current placement left, I was done. I can't do this anymore. It's just too hard.
Later that day, Kristen Welch, author of the blog "We Are That Family" wrote a post and published it the same day. The title of the entry? For When We Are Too Tired To Keep Going. The section that made my eyes well up said...

"How many challenging marriages and hard parenting seasons and difficult jobs and acts of wild obedience have

worn us out and begged us to walk away? Let's face it, sometimes quitting is easier. But often, digging in and pushing past our weariness is where we meet a holy God that says, *'Come unto me and lay your burden down.'*"

And then He fills our arms with Blessings and says, "This is why you must not stop."

So that was timely. And then, later that same day, author Ann Voskamp blogged about their journey over the past year and about their road to adoption. Yeah, I cried some more.

"Sometimes — The story isn't going how you planned, *but that isn't a reason to stop trusting that the story has a plan.* **Sometimes, turns out? You clearly not being enough - is what makes the enoughness of God most clearly seen."**

Oh for the love...okay I get it already. God was speaking to me through a bazillion ways, and I was not going to make the mistake of ignoring him.

So, I won't quit. I will keep on, trusting that my not being enough is what shows Jesus most clearly to others, and trusting for these little ones, and that our God is just and merciful and provides all we need.

Maybe you haven't ever felt this way, or maybe you have - but if you reach a day that you do, I want you to earmark this journal page and come back to it and then I want you to flip to the front two pages where I had you write down your why and your fears and then I want you to pray. It may be time to be done, or it may be time to push through. Only your family can make that decision, but promise yourself not to quit because of fear. Reflect on this, and write down what it going on in your heart right now.

Good Times

"My favorite part about being a foster brother is getting to be nice to the kids. The hardest part is being nice to the kids."- Christian, age 6

For every heavy and hard moment, there are a million good ones. Yes these kids are in care and yes the situation is not ideal, but it is okay to find joy in it and to even seek it out. There is an excitement before a placement comes to your home, the scramble to get all the necessary items, and the anticipation of meeting a precious face. You get to play a fabulous role in the life of a child, and witness so many firsts and crucial moments. You may witness their first teeth, their first steps and their first words. I remember recording with my phone so many firsts, because I knew the family would want to have them, but I knew I'd also want to be able to recall these days.

There is this pitter patter I get when I see a child hug tight to the nape of my husband's neck. We had a placement that, upon seeing my husband pull up the driveway returning from work, began yelling loudly "DADDY!!!" and giggling with delight. That moment was pure joy and I will treasure it.

We took one of our little ones to the Pacific Ocean and seeing the wonder in his eyes was pure magic. The sand in his toes and the awe of the waves left him speechless for a short while.

Seeing our extended family and friends love and accept our little ones is another area of great joy. Our village shows up for birthday parties and exciting moments, and it's as if they had always been a part of us.

I heard our foster daughter singing all of the bedtime songs we sing to her while rocking her babies to sleep and I thought, *This is a safe place and she feels safe and she is modeling that.* And there is joy there. If I am not careful I will get so worn down by the emotions of it all that I will forget to have fun, to be a fun parent, and look for opportunities to celebrate. I don't want to miss out on the good stuff because of the behind the scenes battles that rage. I get to choose joy and I get to teach our children that as well.

Grab a pen and start writing down all of your favorite parts about fostering. Write them all down. The "first" moments you experience, the breakthroughs, the simple victories, the snuggles of a new baby and the first night slept all the way through...write them all down and then earmark this page. Just as writing down things we are thankful for brings us joy, this list will bring you encouragement and hope on the darker days.

A Goodbye Letter

"The burden of foster care does not outweigh the blessing of these children coming into your lives."
- Chelsea, Tennessee Foster Mom

We knew your time with us would be temporary. We knew that whether it was a month or a year, at some point we would say goodbye to you. We knew it would hurt. We knew that it would be difficult no matter when the goodbye happened, but we also knew there would be no way to fully prepare for it.

I will never forget when you first arrived. I can only imagine what was going on in your head. I think I was just as wide-eyed and curious as you were. The days that followed were such a blur, I'm thankful I documented your days with pictures. My, how you've changed.

You learned so much while you were here. It was our joy to watch you blossom.

We want you to know, you were afforded everything our own children were while you were with us. Every bit as much love, every bit as much care, and every bit as much prayer. Often said through tears.

You were tended to with care and concern during the health and sickness while you were here. You were a part of our holiday traditions, our time with our best friends, and birthday parties. You were a part of our training for races, church life, and everything else. You were never treated like anything other than a child of ours.

We did not hold back in our love, or in our fervent prayers for you, or in our supplying you with everything you needed. You have not wanted for anything we were capable of offering. We have asked the Lord to intercede on your behalf. We have asked Him to protect you and to draw you to Himself. We have asked that no matter where you go from our home, you will know deep in your soul that you were loved here and, that as deep as our love for you goes, the Father loves you that much more. We pray you will seek Him and find Him in the days ahead.

I want you to know that our own children loved you. They have never treated you like anything other than a sibling. Whether that was good or bad, it was true. They've been protective of you, thoughtful about you, and they have loved you with a love that we had never seen. You taught them how to love in a whole new way and they are more like Jesus because of it.

You will leave a void in our hearts. My heart is already breaking into a million pieces at the thought of you not being with us, but I do not regret for one moment saying yes to this and yes to you. You are worth the pain in my heart. You are worth the sacrifice we've made to love you big and hard and without strings attached. You deserved to be loved so much that it hurts. You are not a mistake, or an accident, or a problem. You are precious. You have a hope and a future and we are grateful to have played even just a small part in your life.

You, my sweet one...you changed us. You showed us what it really means to have our hearts broken for the things that break the heart of Jesus. You have shown us that it is possible for things to be hard and good and ugly and beautiful all at the same time. Your little life matters.

We will grieve you. It will not be pretty, but we will do this again for another, because there are more of you out there that deserve to be loved. And we will pray that others who have watched us open our hearts and home to you will choose to say "yes" as well, because there are so many like you who need to be loved hard and fully, and we will tell them...it is so worth it.

You are so worth it.

I wrote this letter before our first foster son left. It was a way of processing and expressing my heart for this little one. I don't know your situation or if goodbye is in your future, but if it is - don't let it come without writing down a letter to your foster child as well. You can even use my letter and adjust as you need. Writing down how you feel in this time is a great way to process and can bring healing.

Defender

Defender:
1. a person who defends someone or something
2. synonyms: protector, guard, guardian, preserver; watchdog, keeper, overseer

I can't say we will always have foster kids in our home. I can't say I will always be rocking someone else's child to sleep, kissing their owies, snuggling away their sadness, or praying over them at night. I can't say I will always be in this middle parent role, but what I can say, most definitively, is that I will be defending these children for the rest of my life. I will advocate for them. I will fight for them with my written word, my mouth, and on my knees. I will push for a broken system to be mended, rights to be upheld, and for redemption. I will fight and plead the cause of vulnerable children who have no voice because there is no such thing as "someone else." That someone is me.

I think about Jesus and how He fights for us and is our defender. I think about the unseen battles that go on over the course of my life, and I think about how Jesus shows up again and again when I am weak and worn and unable to muster the strength any longer.
I will model Jesus in foster care, because the need is great and He has already told me what to do.

I bought myself a key with the word defender on it. I wear it around my neck as a reminder to me, to these children. It has also become a great conversation piece. There is something about tangibly putting it over my neck every day as a symbol of what I am doing that helps empower me. You might consider doing something similar, but this week consider writing the word on your wrist as a reminder. Because you are a Defender. On the following page write down everything that comes to mind when you think of a defender.

What Yes Does

You never know where your yes will lead, or what it may produce. We had no idea of the impact that our yes would have on so many different people over the years. We have seen families choose to foster; we have seen families get involved with local non-profits that support foster families; we have seen so many people choose to donate their gently used clothes and toys to the foster parent closet instead of a thrift store. We have seen "Welcome Boxes" stack up in our church entrance for kids coming into care, and we have heard people say, "We watched you and thought, if you can do this we can too."

We may never see the full impact of our yes on this side of heaven, but every now and then you will get a glimpse of glory.

One of our placements had a sibling preparing to make his entrance into the world. While we knew adoption wasn't for us at that time, his mom made the hard loving choice to seek that path. In a crazy, beautiful, sacred web of God moments, our friends ended up adopting this baby at birth. So, in a story only God can write, there will be a forever connection to our former foster son, his mom and this little boy, born to a woman who loved him so much, and was chosen by a Mother and Father who would raise him alongside their other children, knowing what a perfect gift he was.

This piece of grace is one I share often, because it has impact and has ripples that are far more reaching than I could ever fathom.

You just have no idea where your yes will lead, but I believe there is a wild adventure ahead of you when you say it.

Today I want you to think about your own story. Where has your yes led you? Where has it led others? Can you connect any dots yet? Maybe someone you know donated clothes to the foster parent closet instead of a resale store because of your yes. Maybe a family made a frozen meal for another foster family because of your yes. Think hard about it today and take time to track these little threads and see how many you can come up with.

The following section includes prayers and
scriptures to reflect on

A Prayer for the Kids who Come into your Care

Jesus, you have formed each one of these lives, crafted perfectly and wonderfully. You knew where their story would take them. None of this is a surprise to you. Father, we pray for these precious children today. We pray our home would be a safe haven from the storm that surrounds them. We pray that you would hide them in the shadow of your wings, and that you, Almighty God, would move in their lives in a powerful way. We pray for protection, healing and restoration in their lives, and that they would come to know you as their Savior. We pray for the weight that they carry with them, a weight they were not meant to carry. Would you carry their burdens, bring joy to their hearts in the midst of chaos, and surround them with your love- the kind of love that is unfailing, always faithful, a love that never disappoints. May our home be a place where there is refuge and grace. Jesus, we pray the nights would be filled with sweet dreams and the mornings with great hope. Amen.

Psalm 9:9-10 "*The Lord is a shelter for the oppressed, a refuge in times of trouble. Those who know your name trust in you, for you, O Lord, do not abandon those who search for you.*" **NLT**

A Prayer for Social Workers

Jesus, we pray for the men and women on the front lines daily in this foster care world. We pray for the social workers who walk into situations of devastation and trauma on a daily basis. We may see only a few of these faces over our lifetime, but they see so many more. We pray that you would give them soft hearts, strength to do the hard work before them, and to remain tender hearted amidst the very real and scary situations they enter into regularly. We pray you help them find rest and joy and rejuvenation often, so they can continue this difficult, but necessary, task. We pray that you would allow our family to show grace, even when we are frustrated, support even when we disagree, reminding us these people are doing your work, whether they know it or not. Give us incredible amounts of grace for them, trusting they play a part in Your work. We pray for the families they return home to each evening, protect them, and give them hope. Father, thank you for allowing us to partner with them in this work. Amen.

Ephesians 3:16 "*I pray that from his glorious, unlimited resources he will empower you with inner strength through his Spirit.*" **NLT**

A Prayer for the Parents

Jesus, we pray for the precious families of the little ones we care for. We see ourselves in the pain and brokenness represented, and we know that it is only because of your grace we are not in their same situation. We pray you would meet them where they are, call to them in the depths of their souls. May they feel your love and grace through our actions and the way we choose to engage them. We pray they would know how we support them and their efforts, that we are cheering for their reunification if at all possible, and that they are loved. We pray for healing, restoration, and redemption. We pray that you would make something beautiful out of the dust, Father. We pray that no matter our personal feelings towards them, we would choose to love and honor them. Help us to move closer, to embrace the mess of it all, and risk our hearts with love. God, at the end of the day we want them to know you. We want them to find you at the end of their ropes and we trust in that. May we honor them in front of their children and our friends, gracious in deed and word. Amen.

Romans 15:13 *"I pray that God, the source of hope, will fill you completely with joy and peace because you trust in him. Then you will overflow with confident hope through the power of the Holy Spirit."* **NLT**

A Prayer for Your Marriage

Jesus, we know that when we step into your work and say yes to the hard things we open ourselves up to an enemy who wants nothing more than to destroy the work you are doing. We realize there is a very real spiritual threat to our family when we engage in Kingdom work. We pray protection over our marriage; we pray that you would help us to communicate often and well. We pray that you would help us to create margin in our lives to continue be close to one another. We know we cannot do this well if we are not on the same page. We trust in your faithfulness to provide what is needed to carry out the tasks before us. We pray for joy, for love and the gift of time with one another. We pray that you would bind us together, drawing us deeper into an understanding of the love you have for us and the love we have for each other. Protect us from temptation, and prevent little things from being allowed to drive a wedge between us. Thank you for continuing to teach us about your love through our covenant, may we honor one another and in doing so, honor You.

Ephesians 4:2 *"Always be humble and gentle. Be patient with each other, making allowance for each other's faults because of your love."* **NLT**

A Prayer for Safety

Jesus we know that entering into Kingdom work is not to be taken lightly. There are real lives at risk and souls to be won and we don't pretend it will be without casualty. We pray for protection over our family. We pray that you would guard us from temptation, guilt, burn out, and fear. We pray for our physical and mental health, as well as our safety. We believe in a very real battle being waged, and we commit to arming ourselves in prayer and in scripture on a daily basis, trusting that you are in control. You have called us to your work and you will equip us as necessary. Help us to be on guard in all things, alert to our surroundings, both physical and spiritual. We pray protection over these children during their stay with us and when they leave our home. We trust you in all things. Amen.

Psalm 91:4 *"He will cover you with his feathers. He will shelter you with his wings. His faithful promises are your armor and protection."* **NLT**

A Prayer for Strength

Jesus, we are feeling weary. We know this is what you have called us to, but we feel the weight of it all so much. It is crushing. We are in desperate need for a strength only you can provide. Give us rest, give us peace of mind, and help us to create margin in our lives that provides respite and renewal. We don't pretend to be capable of this without you and if we are needing a season of rest from foster care, please make that clear. If we are to carry on in this work, then we need you to move in a powerful way. We cannot keep the pace and be faithful in showing grace and love in this current state. Give us clear wisdom in healthy next steps, give us moments of peace that comes from you and give us the strength we need, be it minute by minute or hour by hour. Help us to learn from you, and hide away, when we can, to renew and restore. Thank you Jesus, for your faithfulness and guidance and power. Amen.

Isaiah 40:29 "*He gives power to the weak and strength to the powerless.*" **NLT**

A Prayer for your Forever Children

Jesus, we pray for our forever children, the ones who were born to us or chosen in adoption, the ones that remain while all the other children come and go. We know that foster care is something we chose and our children are along for the ride. We pray this would teach them to be selfless and compassionate, expand their world God. May they see beyond the bubble of safety they live in and have a deeper knowledge of the world as a whole. We pray for humility and love to be so present in their lives at such a young age that they would be leaders in their schools, teams and social groups. We pray blessing upon them. These kids give up much more than we often realize and often with gracious hearts. We pray you would just pour out abundant blessing on them. Our children are our partners in this and we pray protection over them. We pray that they would find you Jesus in such deep and intimate way, and despite their age they would know deep in their hearts who you are. We pray that they would see modeled a life of saying yes to hard things, even when we are afraid. We pray, as their foster siblings come and go, you would protect their hearts from the often unseen grief and comfort them. Thank you for allowing us the privilege of raising world changers. Help us to do it well. Amen.

1 Timothy 4:12 "*Don't let anyone think less of you because you are young. Be an example to all believers in what you say, in the way you live, in your love, your faith, and your purity.*" **NLT**

Trace the Hand

Here you will find a few blank pages to trace the hands of the little ones who come and go from your care. My hope is that you would place your hand over theirs as you pray over them after they have gone. It will be a bittersweet and precious spot to treasure over the years and no doubt the pages will turn color from the oils in your fingers and the tears that drop to the pages. Feel free to stick in extra pages if you run out.

Matthew 19:15 "*And he placed his hands on their heads and blessed them before he left.*" **NLT**

The leaves, having done their job of providing for the tree, one

by one let go and take flight.

The day will come when I will let go of you and a little part of

me will wither inside.

I know I will have done what was needed for a season and just

like the dead leaves continue to provide

long after they have fallen, enriching the soil below…

I pray our time together brings strength that you carry with you

into the unknown.

Acknowledgements

I have the best village of people anyone could ever hope for. Thank you can hardly contain my gratitude. Thank you to my sweet man and my biggest fan, Trevor. Watching you be Dad to other children has not only made me fall madly in love with you all over again, it has made me that much more thankful our kids have you as an example. Thank you for pushing me, encouraging me and picking up the slack around the home while I worked like mad at my computer. You're my very best friend and I think you're hot. Jack, Camden and Christian you amaze me. Your kindness, love and sacrifice has taught me so much. Thank you for opening your hearts and your rooms for children who need a safe place. I get giddy when I think about what you will do with this in the future. Mom and Dad, you show up again and again with love, support and encouragement and you've played the role of Nama and Capa beautifully to our foster children. Thank you for teaching me what a life of service looks like, you are the best. To my sister, Breanna, I love you. Thank you for your consistent support and concern with whatever our family is doing, and your willingness to love where we love. Jenna Benton, it feels inadequate to refer to you as just my writing coach. You are the one who challenged me to get this out into the hands of others. You guided me gently, with kindness and wisdom and pushed me to be a better writer and always had "carrots" dangling in front of me to keep me going. I love you immensely. To my gracious and wicked smart editors, Carolyn Thompson and Alisha Vosburg. Thank you for being willing to take on this project amidst your busy lives and offer such encouragement in the process. This wouldn't be here without you. To Shawn Sampson who never lets me settle on a surface answer, who makes me mad with probing questions but has pushed me to better myself and my "why", thank you for your friendship, your help in making sure things aligned theologically and for designing this beautiful cover. To Amy, thank you for your belief in me, in so many areas, thank you for stepping out in faith and leading the way, thank you for answering my crazy helpless texts with encouragement, advice and hope. Thank you for loving me when I'm crazy. To my amazing group of foster Moms who keep me sane, Leah, Christina, Crystal, Laurie and my insta-friend Chelsie. Thank you for your friendship and for lending your voice to this book. You are doing beautiful work and I'm honored to be a part of it. Thank you Dale for your scripture suggestions and theological guidance. Thank you to Adriel Booker and Tam Hodge for believing these words needed to be shared. To Shirley Nelson, my 4th grade teacher who told me I was a writer. I am grateful to be a part of a church body who believes the Jesus Way happens outside of our walls and invests in the lives of those in our community and around the world.

CPSIA information can be obtained
at www.ICGtesting.com
Printed in the USA
FSHW020953220121
77902FS